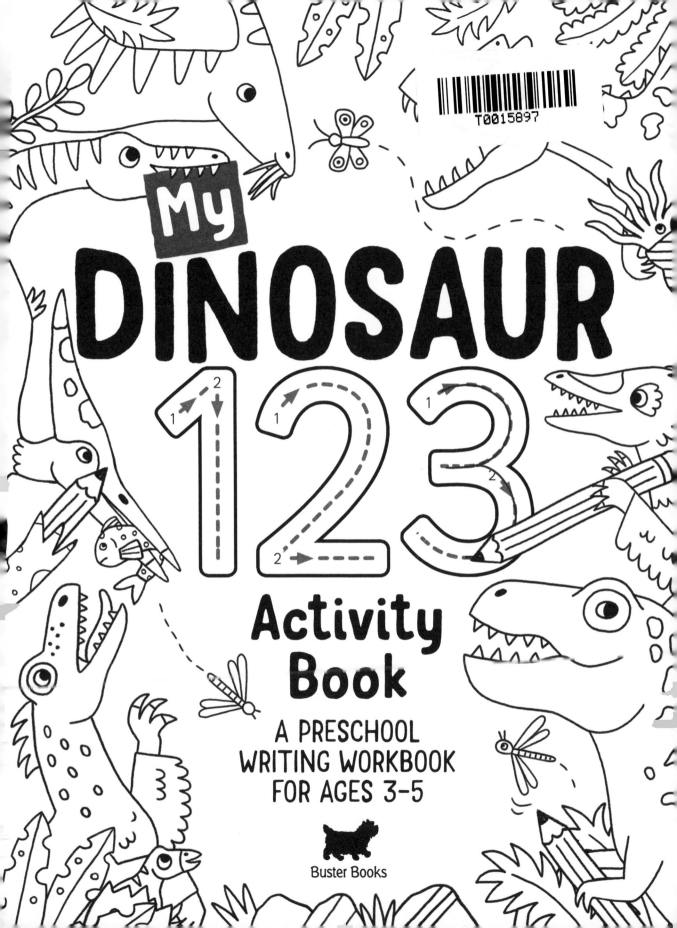

My DINOSAUR 123

Activity Book

A PRESCHOOL WRITING WORKBOOK FOR AGES 3-5

Buster Books

Illustrated by Sophie Foster

Edited by Josephine Southon
Cover designed by Jade Moore
Designed by Jack Clucas

First published in Great Britain in 2022 by Buster Books, an imprint of
Michael O'Mara Books Limited, 9 Lion Yard, Tremadoc Road, London SW4 7NQ

W www.mombooks.com/buster   f Buster Books   🐦 @BusterBooks   📷 @buster_books

ISBN: 978-1-78055-854-7

1 3 5 7 9 10 8 6 4 2

This book was printed in May 2022 by
Shenzhen Wing King Tong Paper Products Co. Ltd.,
Shenzhen, Guangdong, China.

FSC
www.fsc.org   MIX
Paper | Supporting
responsible forestry
FSC® C010256

How To Use This Book

This book will teach your child how to write from 1 to 20, in numbers and in words.

Encourage your child to follow the numbered arrows in order, tracing over the dashed lines in the direction the arrows are pointing. For example:

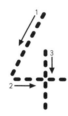

The guidelines fade with each new attempt. There is blank space at the end of the line to practise forming the number or word. There is also space at the back of the book for extra practice.

There are lots of friendly dinosaurs and prehistoric creatures to meet along the way. A pronunciation guide at the back shows how to say their names.

1

one

a Spinosaurus has 1 sail

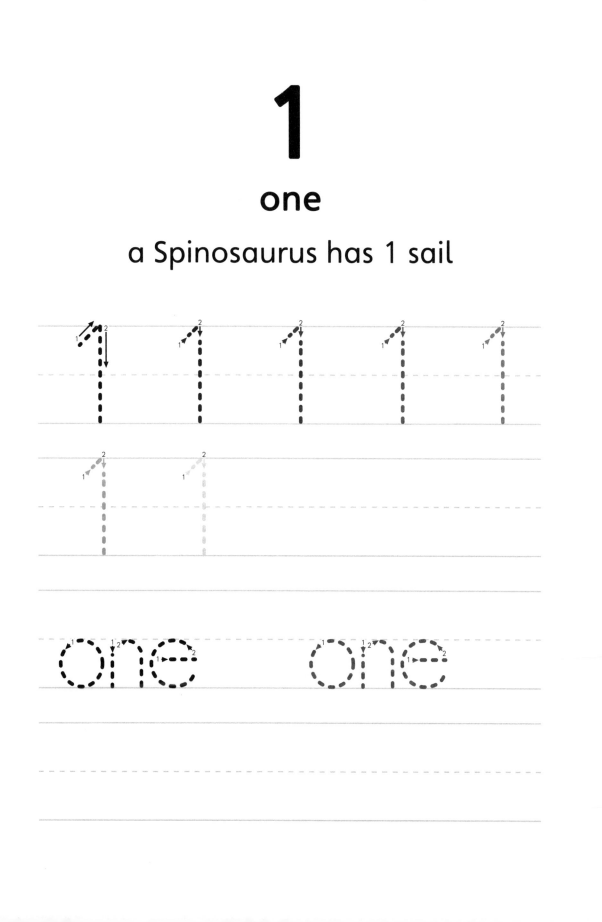

2

two

a Tyrannosaurus has 2 arms

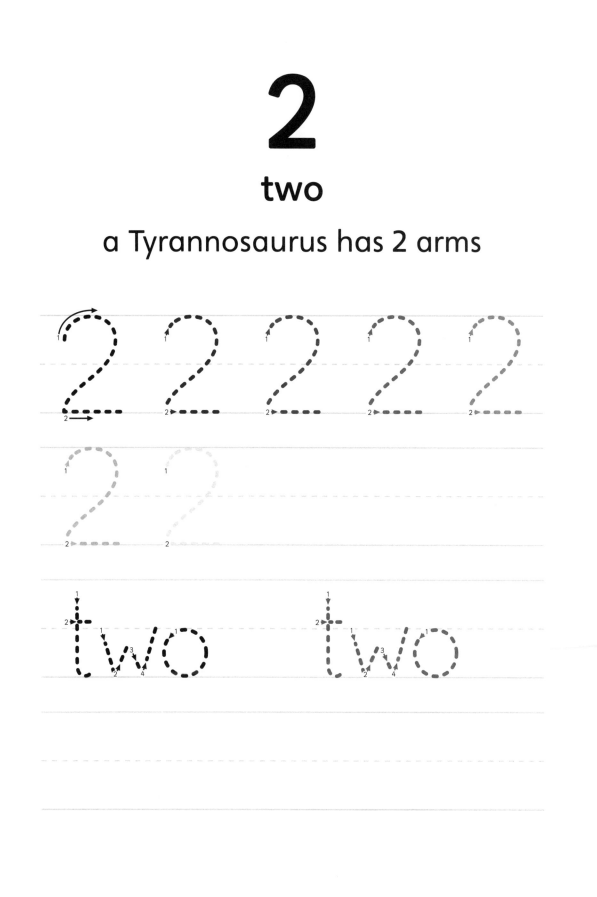

3

three

a Triceratops has 3 horns

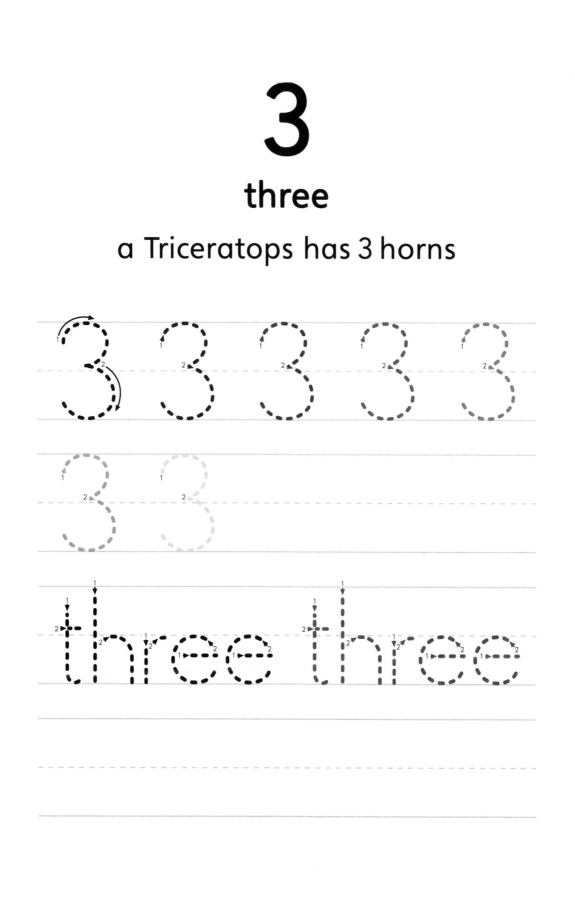

4

four

a plesiosaur has 4 flippers

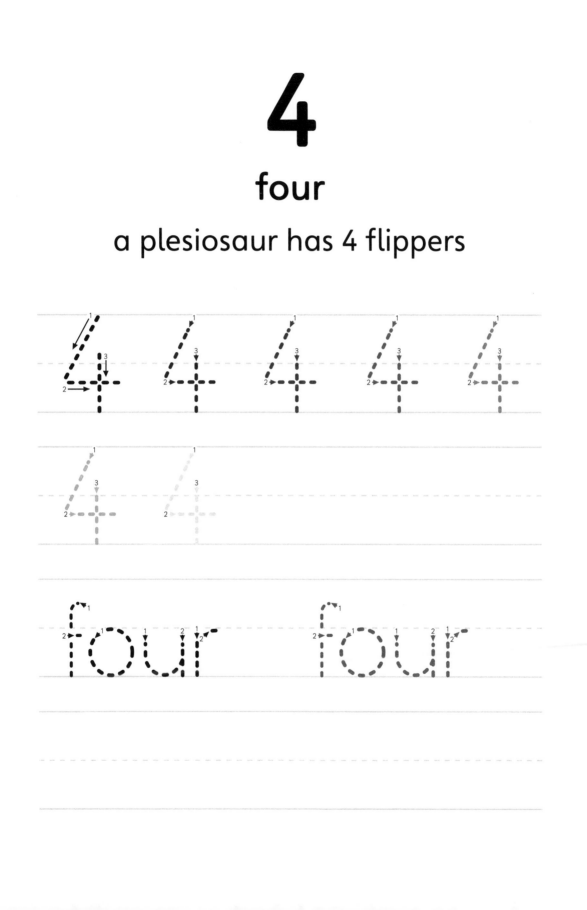

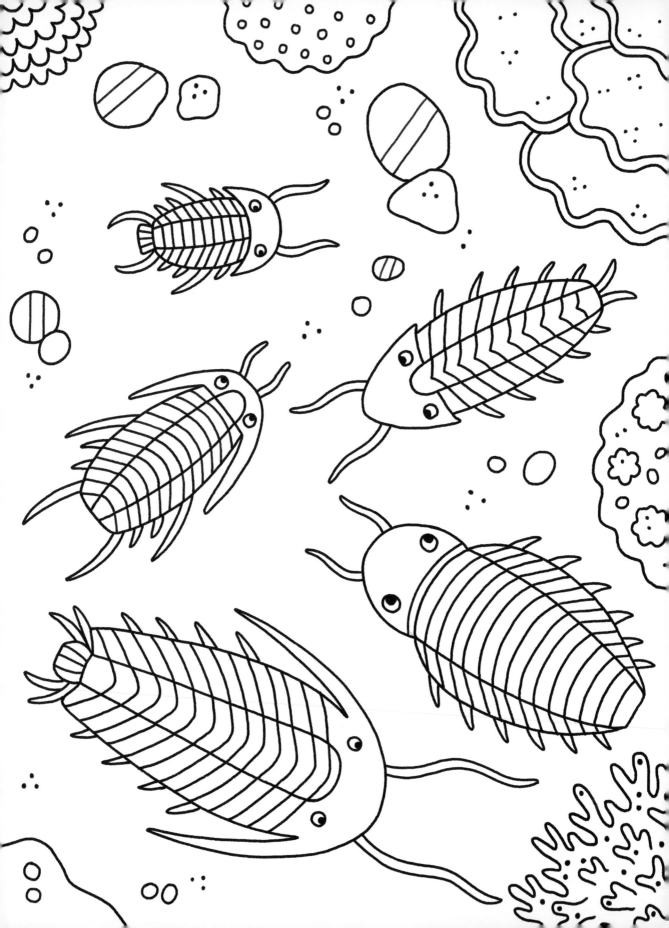

5

five

5 trilobites are crawling on the seabed

6

six

6 ammonites are swimming in the ocean

7

seven

7 volcanoes are erupting

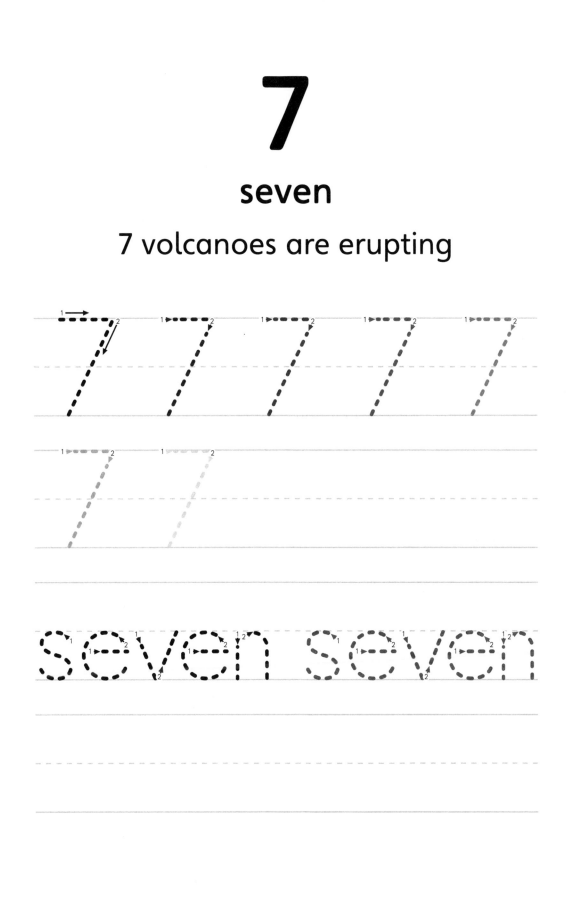

8

eight

an Ankylosaurus has made 8 footprints

9

nine

a Styracosaurus has 9 spikes

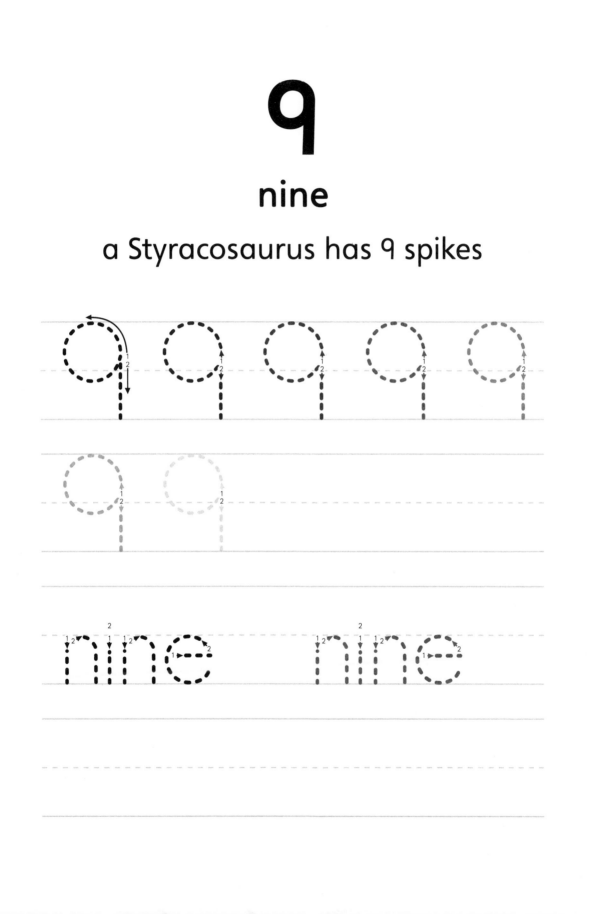

10

ten

a Pterodactylus has found 10 fish

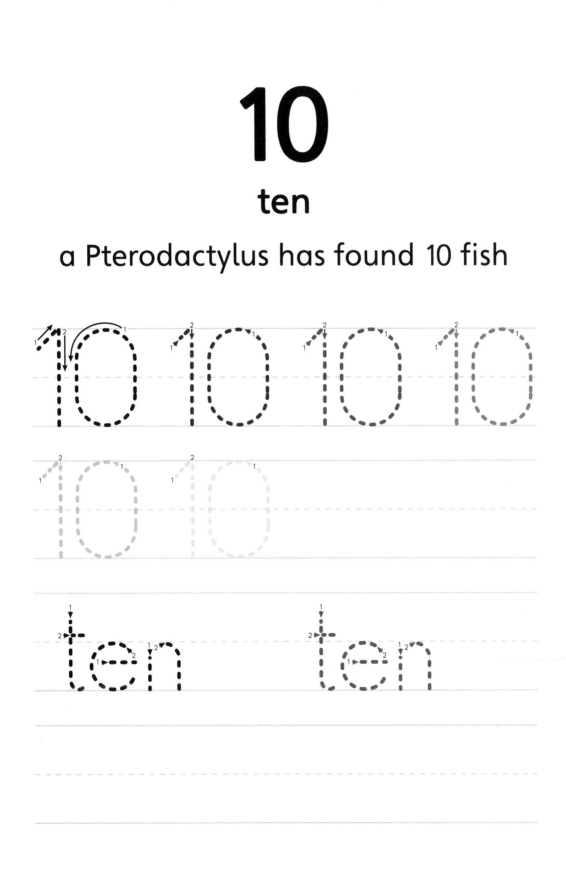

11

eleven

there are 11 meteors in the sky

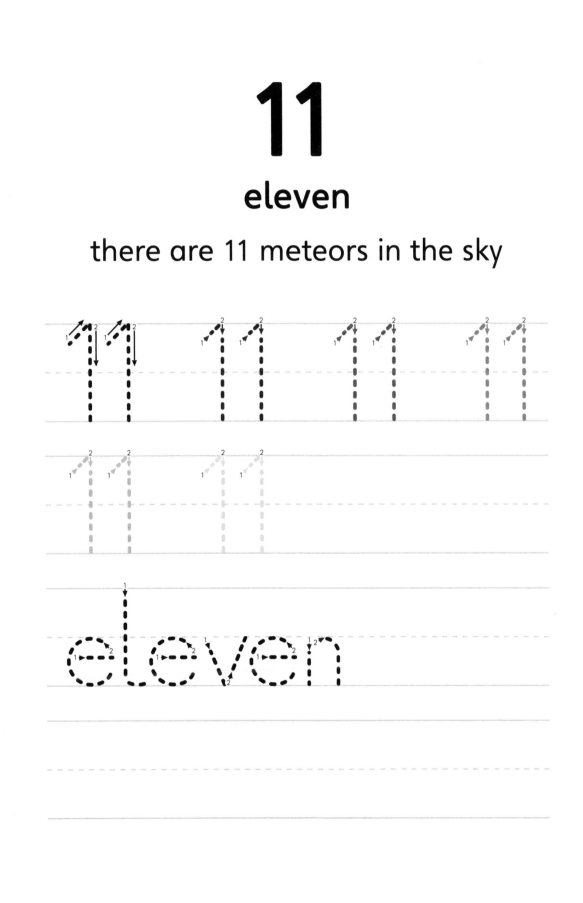

12

twelve

this Diplodocus has 12 spots

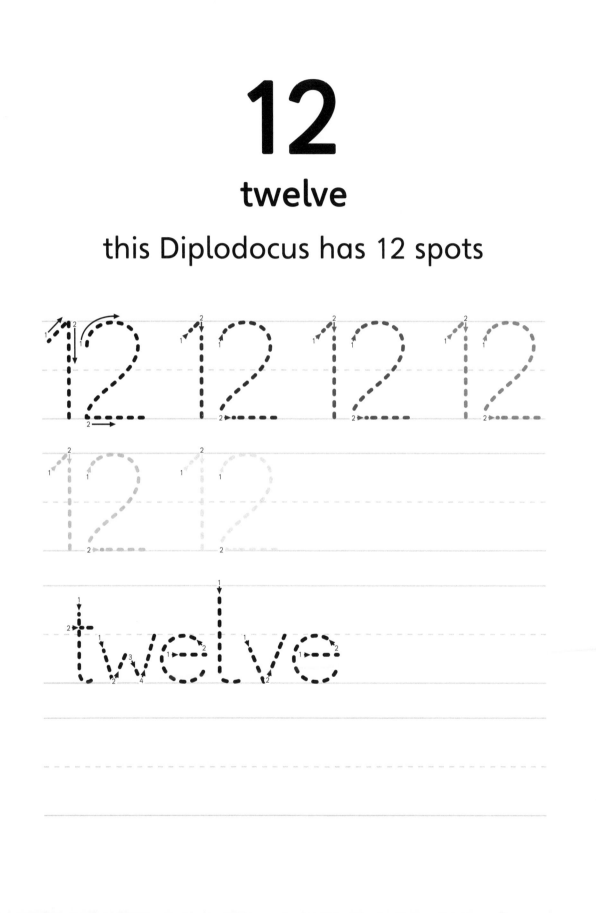

13

thirteen

this Apatosaurus has 13 stripes

14

fourteen

there are 14 hadrosaur in this herd

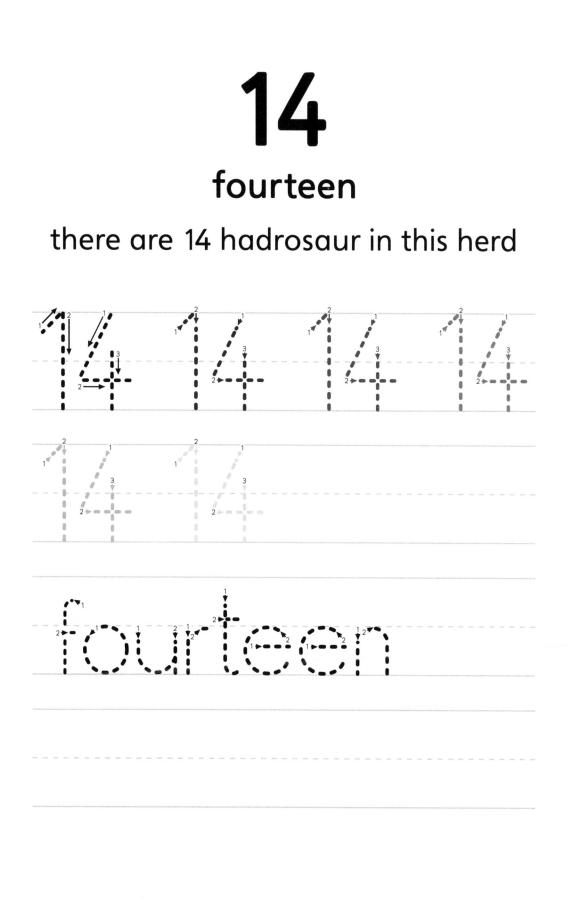

15

fifteen

15 Meganeura flutter their wings

16

sixteen

a Parasaurolophus has found 16 ferns to eat

17

seventeen

a Stegosaurus has 17 plates on its back

18

eighteen

this Triassic forest has 18 trees

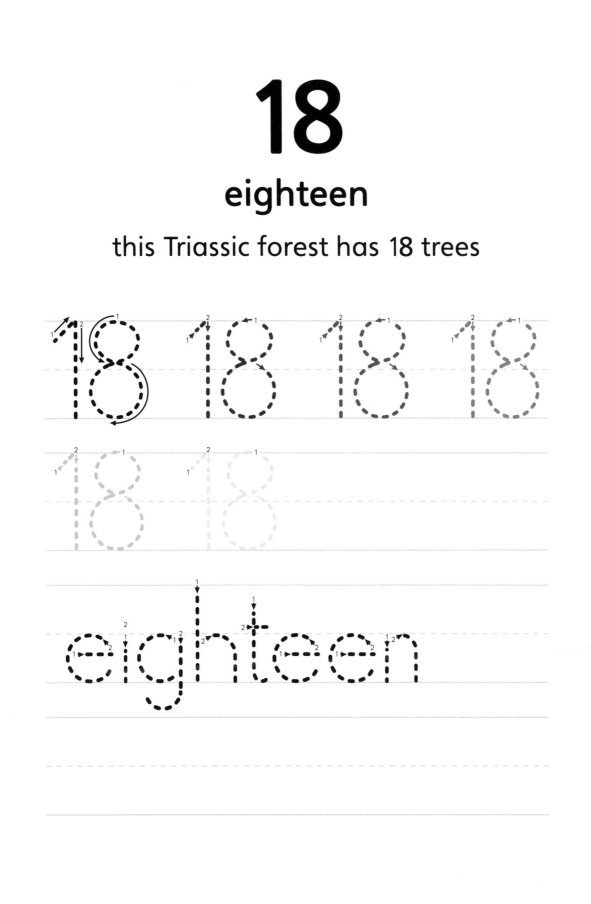

19

nineteen

a Velociraptor is munching on 19 bones

20

twenty

an Oviraptor has laid 20 eggs

1
sail

2 arms

3 horns

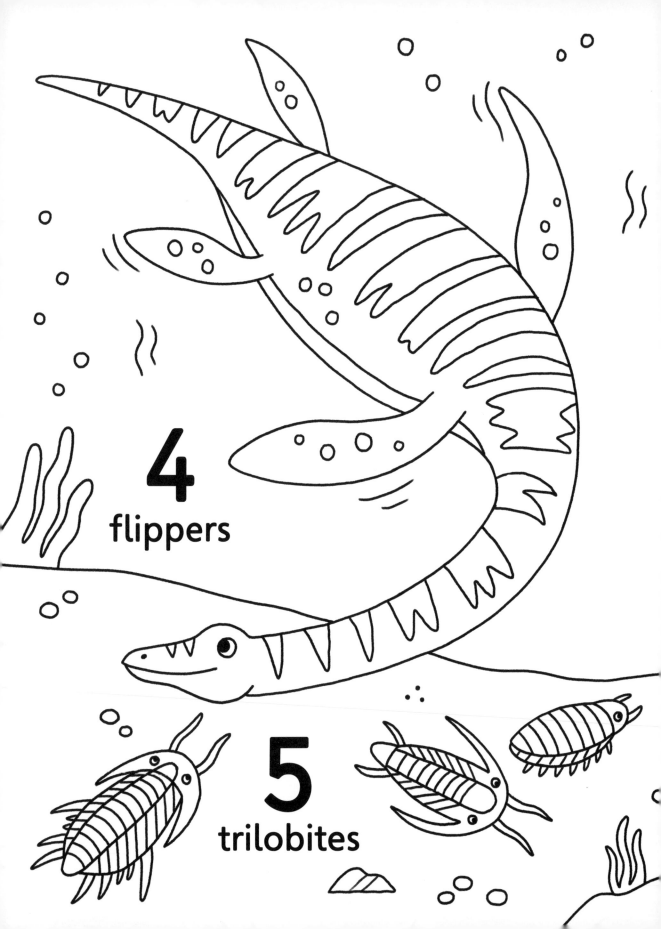

4
flippers

5
trilobites

6
ammonites

7
volcanoes

8
footprints

9

spikes

11
meteors

10
fish

12
spots

13 stripes

14 hadrosaur

15
Meganeura

16
ferns

18 trees

17 plates

19
bones

20
eggs

Extra writing practice

Pronunciation guide

Some of the names in this book can be tricky to say. Use this guide to help you.

Spinosaurus: spy-nuh-sore-us

Tyrannosaurus: tie-ran-oh-sore-us

Triceratops: try-sair-uh-tops

Plesiosaur: pless-ee-oh-sore

Trilobite: try-luh-bite

Ammonite: am-on-ite

Ankylosaurus: an-kie-loh-sore-us

Styracosaurus: stih-rak-oh-sore-us

Pterodactylus: teh-roh-dack-till-us

Diplodocus: dih-plod-oh-kus

Apatosaurus: ah-pat-oh-sore-us

Hadrosaur: had-roe-sore

Meganeura: meg-ah-new-ra

Parasaurolophus: pa-ra-sore-rol-off-us

Stegosaurus: steg-oh-sore-us

Velociraptor: vel-oss-ee-rap-tor

Oviraptor: oh-vee-rap-tor